The Fortune-Telling Book

Also in this series:

The Good Spell Book

Love Charms, Magical Cures, and Other Practical Sorcery

THE FORTUNE-TELLING BOOK

by

Gillian Kemp

READING

CRYSTAL BALLS,

TEA LEAVES,

PLAYING CARDS,

AND EVERYDAY OMENS

OF LOVE AND

LUCK

Little, Brown and Company

Boston New York London

L|B
1837

To my faithful
Yorkshire terrier ~~Daisy May~~,
who passed away on the day
the book was completed.
Her spirit is in its pages.

To my publisher, Amanda,
my agent, Chelsey,
to you, the reader,
to Katie Boyle and also
to the one I love.

Contents

A door that opens itself
        forecasts a visitor.
Guests should always
    leave your home by the door
            they entered.

People have been telling fortunes since time began. You have the power within you to see your own future, or that of your friends, no matter what your age or circumstance. ¶ The ancient art of divination is a vast subject, too large to be covered in its entirety here. This little book shows you simply how to develop your psychic and clairvoyant abilities, and to invoke them to tell fortunes using everyday household items such as tea leaves or coffee grounds, a pack of playing cards, a pair of dice, a bowl of water or ice, candles, or apples. Most likely you already have the ingredients at hand, and because each method is easy to use, you can begin anytime you like. Also included here are everyday omens and superstitions that have stood the test of time. ¶ Once your mind is receptive to higher influences, you will find there is far more to life than just what meets the eye. You've probably already had the experience of knowing who is on the telephone before you pick up the receiver. Or perhaps you have thought of someone and then heard from that person or bumped into her, or had a hunch or a feeling that something would happen. Your intuition is the compass that will always point you in the right direction. The door is already open; dare you step through?

Otherwise they will depart with your good luck.

If you want to be rich,
position the head of your bed
in the east, and sleep in that
position. If you desire to travel,
place the head of your bed
in the west.

TUNING
YOUR MIND

Clairvoyance is special sight (literally, it means "clear sight") that allows you to see the future in a crystal ball or a teacup. If you can think of a lemon, see its shape and color, cut it in half and smell its aroma in your mind, you have clairvoyant powers. If not, you can become clairvoyant by training your imagination to visualize an object or situation. ❧ Psychics have the power to feel, such as divining by psychometry (below). You can encourage your psychic powers in a number of ways, often with the help of a friend. The more often you try these methods, the more accurate your predictions will be.

PSYCHIC POWERS

[15]

Try sensing a drawing. Begin by holding out your left palm, flat and face up. While you have your eyes closed, a friend should draw a shape in the air — either a heart shape, a square, a circle, a wavy line, or a cross — about an inch or two above your palm. Your challenge is to sense which shape they have drawn.

TELEPATHY

Telepathy is thought transference, or communication between minds using extrasensory means. ❧ Take a deck of playing cards. Remove all the face cards so that you are left with numbers one to ten in each suit.

Shuffle the remaining forty cards (twenty will be red and twenty black) and pass them to a friend. ¶ The pair of you should then sit back to back. Ask your friend to remove the top card and telepathically convey to you the number on the card and the color of the card. The pair of you should continue until the pack has been exhausted. Again, the more often you try, the more accurate you will become.

PSYCHOMETRY

Psychometry is the divination of facts about a person via his or her possessions. ¶ To intuit a friend's feelings or details from their past, present, or future, ask to hold an item of their jewelry, such as a watch or ring. Hold it with your eyes closed for a few moments. Because the item has absorbed your friend's aura — the distinctive energy emanating from their body — you should be able to make a prediction in only five minutes. ¶ Another method is to hold to your forehead a letter or card someone has sent. You will detect their mood, character, and the surroundings in which the letter was written.

CRYSTAL BALL READING

Otherwise known as Crystalomancy or Scrying

The word crystal is of Greek origin and means "clear ice," or "frozen water." The genuine article is quartz crystal, mined from the earth. If you buy a crystal, ask whether it is real quartz; a label saying "genuine crystal" can actually mean genuine glass crystal, which usually has tiny air bubbles inside and a tinge of sulphur yellow color.

Reading a crystal ball is easy — it requires only imagination and concentration. If you can see pictures in the clouds when you look at the sky, you have the power to see pictures in a crystal ball, or in an ice cube or a bowl of clean water instead. ¶ The best time of day for scrying is sunset, or any time that does not need electric lighting. The best time of the month for scrying is when the moon is waxing (becoming full), because a quartz crystal is ruled by the moon, and because clairvoyant and psychic powers increase with the waxing moon. You should never read a crystal ball after midnight, because it will attract and reveal darker forces. ¶ When you are reading a crystal ball for a friend, have them hold the ball in their left hand or place the globe on a table in a metal or wooden stand. If you like candlelight, keep a lit candle behind you. Place the ball on a plain black or dark blue velvet cloth or silk scarf, to help eliminate reflections from the room. You don't want to see reflections, but rather a complete blank, something empty waiting to be filled. ¶ If the ball is on a table, the person may sit beside or opposite you, but they need to be close. If they are holding the ball in their left hand, they need to sit on your right, perhaps on a sofa or wherever you both will be comfortable for about ten or twenty

[19]

If you don't have a crystal ball, use a bowl of water or a bowl of ice.

SEE HYDROMANCY, BELOW

minutes. ¶ Place the crystal in your friend's left hand so that his fingers clutch without obscuring the ball. Place one of your hands under his left hand. The ball is heavy, so rest the cupped ball on his lap or on yours. Clear your mind and gaze into the center of the ball. Try not to force visions, but allow apparitions to appear to you. Within a couple of minutes, the ball will become cloudy or milky, which means a vision is about to appear. ¶ Visions will float into the ball from any direction, rather like a cloud in the sky. Because the mist is in motion, you will need to give a running commentary on what you are seeing. [20] You may visualize objects, people, animals, or events. A crystal ball cannot indicate time, so unless you note specific seasonal themes, what you see may either be the near or distant future. ¶ Move your gaze from the center of the crystal, where details of the scene increase. The picture will build up until it fills the ball. When you have described all that you see, refocus your vision on the center of the ball. The former picture will have disappeared and a new vision will begin to emerge. ¶ During a reading, you should always make statements, never pose questions. The person receiving a reading should listen without speaking. When you eventually refocus on the center of the crystal and the picture is unchanged, the energy is fading, and the reading is coming to an end. ¶ Conclude your reading by asking if your friend would like you to answer a question about his future. When the question has been asked, look into the center of the crystal again. You may see another image in the ball, or the answer may just pop into your mind, because your aura has been blending with the thoughts of the person holding the crystal. ¶ Afterward, always rinse the ball under cold or tepid running tap water, and when putting it away, wrap it in a silk scarf or velvet square.

[21]

If you are using a quartz crystal ball, you can recharge its energy by exposing the crystal to a few hours of moonlight during three nights when the moon is becoming full, or on the night of a full moon, but remove the crystal ball before daylight.

TO GIVE YOURSELF
A CRYSTAL BALL
READING

When reading for yourself, visions will appear in exactly the same manner as when you are reading for a friend or stranger. Find a place where you feel most at ease. Light a candle and place it where it will not cast reflections. If you are using a crystal ball, hold the globe in your left hand. Breathe in and out three times, imagining that you are breathing in good energy and exhaling problems. ❦ Once you are relaxed, gaze into the center of the crystal and allow your mind to drift into a daydream state. You are allowed to blink. Images will float into the center of the ball. The more deeply you concentrate, the more detail you will see. Some images may be symbolic, like a key, which might be a key to success or the key to your heart. A key may also mean new doors will open, or foretell moving to a new home. A horseshoe symbolizes good luck. ❦ Continue until you simply feel it's time to finish. Afterward, try making a few notes on what you have predicted for yourself. You will see your prophecies fulfilled. And because crystals absorb the energy of others, you may like to keep a crystal ball for your personal use only.

HYDROMANCY

predicting the future using a bowl of water

It's just as effective to use a bowl of water instead of a crystal ball. Predicting the future with water is perhaps the oldest form of divination that exists. ❧ Place a large, deep glass bowl on the table, which should be covered with a black or dark blue cloth to eliminate reflections in the room. If you have only a small glass bowl, that's fine too. Pour cold tap or bottled water into the bowl until it reaches the brim. Place a lit candle behind your right shoulder and turn off the electric lights, making sure you still have enough light to see. You and your client need to sit close together, and the bowl should be at book-reading distance from both of you. ❧ Be calm, and concentrate for a few moments while you and your client both look into the center of the water. In exactly the same way as when using a crystal ball, misty visions will float in. (For more detail, see above.)

[25]

A VARIATION

If you are using ice instead of a bowl of water, freeze water in a rounded bowl, the larger the better. Turn the ice onto a plate, so the dome shape is facing upward. You will not only see visions in the ice, but you may see images in the water surrounding the ice as it melts.

ANOTHER VARIATION

You can also scry with a far more modern vessel — an empty round shoe polish tin. Paint the base and lid, inside and out, with black paint. When it is dry, fill the base of the tin with cold water and use it in the same way as you would a crystal ball. Replace the lid when not in use and keep it for your magical purpose.

DIVINATION BY WATER

Write your questions on small pieces of paper that are equal in size. Roll the paper into tiny balls. Drop all of them at the same time into an empty bowl. Pour water into the bowl and look quickly. "Yes" is the answer to the question on the first piece of paper that rises to the surface.

USING WATER
TO FORECAST
LOVE

Cut a piece of cardboard into 26 tiny squares and write one of the 26 individual letters of the alphabet on each. Place the squares facedown in a bowl and fill the bowl with water before going to bed. In the morning, the letters that have turned themselves face up indicate initials or letters, which partly or completely spell your next lover's name. ❧ Place a saucer on a table and drop 21 dressmaking needles onto it. Very slowly, pour water from a jug into the saucer. The water will cause the needles to move. Two needles that cross indicate that you have an admirer. You have as many potential lovers as you have crossed needles.

[27]

The Babylonians saw visions in sacred bowls filled with liquid, the Egyptians looked into pools of ink, and the Hindus into bowls of molasses.

APPLE
DIVINATIONS

TO DIVINE THE
LOCATION OF YOUR
FUTURE PARTNER

Place an apple seed in your left hand and cover it with your right. Shake both hands saying:

> *Apple seed, apple seed, of the apple tree,*
> *Tell me where my true love will be.*
> *North, South, East, or West,*
> *Apple seed, apple seed, answer my request.*

Open your palm. The direction in which the pointed end of the seed is facing is the direction in which true love and partnership lie.

[31]

Apples are ruled by the love planet Venus, and can be used to predict matters of the heart.

TO PREDICT
THE FIRST INITIAL
OF THE ONE
YOU WILL MARRY

With each twist of an apple stem, recite a letter in alphabetical order. The letter you reach when the stem breaks is the initial of the Christian name of the person you will marry. To find the initial of his surname, tap the broken end of the stem against the apple while reciting the alphabet. The letter you reach when the stem breaks the apple's skin reveals the answer.

If the hem of your skirt
or leg of your pants accidentally
turns up and stays there,
  forming a pocket shape,

TO DIVINE
WHICH OF TWO
LOVERS LOVES
YOU MOST

Apple seeds can divine who is most deserving of you.
❧ Slice an apple in half and remove two seeds. Name
one seed for one lover and the second seed for your
other lover. With your fingers, press both seeds to
your forehead, remembering which seed symbolizes
which lover. Remove your fingers and the seeds
should stay on your forehead for a few moments. The
first seed to fall from your forehead represents the
lover who least loves you. The seed that sticks to your
forehead for the longest time represents the man
who loves you most and will love you longest.

[33]

you will be given or sent something that will fit in your pocket.

HE LOVES ME?
HE LOVES ME NOT?

To determine whether someone loves you, eat an apple to the core until you find a seed. Remove the seed and name it by the same name as the one you love. ❧ With a pin, inscribe the name of the one you love on a candle. Light the candle and leave it to burn for a few moments before dropping the seed into the candle flame. If the seed makes a cracking sound, the one you desire can hardly contain his feelings for you. Snuff the candle out.

[34]

PLAYING CARDS~
CARTOMANCY

he origin of playing cards is lost in the mists of time. ¶ But most sources agree that playing cards were invented in the Far East. The earliest cards were called *naibe,* which is Arabic and translates as "to foretell." Their primary purpose was for divination; playing games with the cards was an afterthought. ¶ The history of playing cards is as mysterious as the fortunes they tell. It is worth noting there are 52 weeks in the year and 52 cards. There are four suits, symbolic perhaps of the four seasons of the year, the four divisions of a day (morning, afternoon, evening, and night), or the four elements (earth, air, fire, and water). The four suits also harmonize with the stages of life: diamonds signify youth; clubs, adulthood; hearts, maturity; and spades, old age. ¶ Also significant: there are thirteen cards in each suit and thirteen lunar months in a year, as well as thirteen weeks in each quarter of the year. There are twelve court cards (so called because they feature kings, queens, and jacks), and perhaps not just by coincidence there are twelve months in the year and twelve zodiac houses. ¶ Playing cards were first printed from engraved blocks in the fourteenth century. Today's playing cards have remained virtually unchanged for centuries, and still feature the costume of Henry VIII's day. ¶ Because each playing card has a corresponding meaning, cartomancy — telling fortunes with playing cards — is a very versatile way of

[37]

revealing the past, present, and future of your own or another person's life. Cards can predict love, health, wealth, and happiness. They have the ability to forecast generally as well as to answer specific questions, and answers can be found using simple or more complex methods. ¶ Most homes possess a pack of playing cards. Unlike a crystal ball, they are lightweight, easy to carry, and discreet in appearance. Not only can cards help you make up your mind, they can help you make the kind of choices that ensure your future success and happiness. In the same way that your personal pack of playing cards will become an indispensable aid in solving your own dilemmas, your special ability to read cards will draw friends who will depend on you when they have a decision to make or a crisis. Even if they don't believe, people will find you entertaining and will want you at their parties. And by reading the cards for them, you will sharpen your intuitive ability to read people.

[38]

Court cards in red suits (hearts and diamonds) personify fair-haired, fair-skinned people. Dark-haired, dark-skinned people are signified by black cards (clubs and spades).

HOW TO BEGIN

Writing the few key word meanings on each card is a good idea until you know every interpretation by heart. Stopping to refer to the book may disrupt your flow. You may feel more comfortable making a brief forecast and then consulting the book for a more precise reading and a broader perspective. ❡ The two Jokers in the pack should be removed. If you want to add some complexity to the reading, include cards that are reversed—write an "R" upside down in the right-hand corner of each card, which will indicate that the image is upside down—and shuffle them into the pack, making sure that the shuffle does not leave all the cards with an upside down in the right-hand corner. ❡ Each card has its own special meaning, but each of the four suits also has a general significance that will help guide you:

[39]

♥ *Hearts signify love, friendship, and domestic matters. They are happy cards.*

♠ *Spades for the most part symbolize difficulties in life, such as sorrow, treachery, and infidelity.*

♦ *Diamonds denote career, money, and travel.*

♣ *Clubs allude to business.*

But only broadly speaking, as this is a versatile rule.

There are also a few special combinations,
which are helpful to know.

- *Ace of hearts beside a heart*
  Intimates affectionate friendship and true love.
  A friend may become your lover or introduce you
  to someone who falls in love with you.

- *Ace of hearts between two hearts*
  Represents a passionate love affair. Expect the love
  affair you wish for. Someone new may try to steal
  your heart away.

- *Ace of hearts between two diamonds*
  Means expect money. This is likely to be a windfall
  or an expensive gift.

- *Ace of hearts between spades*
  Anticipate quarrels. It may be a lovers' tiff or a
  disagreement with a family member and may cause
  you much heartache.

- *Ten of hearts between spades*
  Casts a rosy glow on the reading and cancels the negative cards on either side of the heart. A problem you
  may have will be resolved to your satisfaction.

- *Ace of spades beside king of clubs*
  Await a meeting with a good, important, influential
  businessman who may offer you reasonably paid work.

- *Ace of spades beside four of hearts*
  The future conception of a baby for someone close.

- *Two aces side by side*
  A happy engagement or marriage for you or someone close if the cards are red. Two black aces reveal loss of money and a broken friendship.

- *Four aces*
  You will experience great happiness and great sadness, success and failure. Somehow you will reconcile the two and gain deep understanding. Your life will be adventurous and exciting, perhaps unusual.

- *Ace of diamonds beside eight of clubs*
  Expect someone to offer a business proposal or a valuable gift.

- *Ten of diamonds between two hearts*
  Anticipate a prosperous marriage, for you or someone close. It may be a wealth of happiness rather than monetary riches.

- *Two of clubs beside two of diamonds*
  Expect brilliant news to grant a heartfelt wish.

[41]

THE **CLUB** SUIT

♣ King

KEY WORDS: *Helpful strong man.*

This card often represents a physically, financially, and mentally mature businessman. Genuinely fond of you and seemingly honorably intentioned, he may offer a partnership, a job, or expert advice, but probably not marriage.

REVERSED: *A miserly man will help you, but only at a price.*

♣ Queen

KEY WORDS: *Supportive tender woman.*

[42] This attractive, confident woman has a maternal nature and many male admirers. Her generosity attracts many friends, and you may confide in her. She may help you to earn a living.

REVERSED: *Be discreet, a woman may be jealous of you.*

♣ Jack

KEY WORDS: *Studious young man.*

This affectionate, flirtatious young man is a bit of a lovable rogue. Hardworking and determined, his great ambitions often bring just rewards. He may influence you to move home or change direction.

REVERSED: *Beware, like all knaves he can be destructive to you and himself through youthful folly.*

The reversed meaning is when the card is upside down.

♣ 1⊙

KEY WORDS: *Money luck.*

A beneficial business transaction will improve your destiny. It may occur in ten days, on the tenth of a month, in ten weeks, or in October. This is a good time to sign contracts or make business investments. You may change your appearance to reflect a new image.

REVERSED: *Travel may be delayed but you will explore new places.*

♣ 9

KEY WORDS: *Immediate opportunities.*

You are very much in control of your fast-track career. A solution to financial difficulties will arrive in nine weeks or in September. Longtime friends will back you and rejoice when you succeed.

REVERSED: *Your situation is unstable. Keep a low profile.*

♣ 8

KEY WORDS: *A successful gamble.*

Renowned as the card of chance, it intimates that you will win a gamble. Follow your intuition, but if sixth sense tells you, stop gambling for a time. An advancement at work will occur on the eighth of a month or in August.

REVERSED: *Avoid foolish speculations. Remember, investments fall as well as rise.*

♣7

KEY WORDS: *Good news.*

The gates to success open for you with the arrival of important business letters or contracts. As your prosperity gains momentum, you will enjoy the pleasures that security and status bring. Success may depend on how you use the number seven in a lottery.

REVERSED: *Neither a lender nor a borrower be.*

♣6

KEY WORDS: *Unexpected financial enrichment.*

[44]

Past business success will generate new work opportunities. Money may come from an unexpected source, but balance income and expenditure cautiously. Keep in touch with people who have advised you wisely in the past. June promises to be a good month for you.

REVERSED: *Expect a good news reply to a letter you send regarding your career.*

♣5

KEY WORDS: *A wealthy marriage.*

The signs are that if you are already relatively well off, your life will continue to be similarly secure. If, however, you are not so lucky, you will have to work hard to fulfill your dreams. A breakthrough will occur in May. If unattached, you may meet a kind lover through work.

REVERSED: *Financial problems evaporate through work.*

♣ 4

KEY WORDS: *Financial instability.*

A decline of financial fortune is indicated. Discuss your problems with valued friends, a bank, or an insurance broker. Before long, fund-raising efforts will be successful. You will hear good news in April.

REVERSED: *Avoid tempting thieves or losing precious items.*

♣ 3

KEY WORDS: *Financial progress.*

A business plan that failed previously now succeeds because you are in the right place at the right time. A long-standing relationship may develop into marriage. Good news and happiness arrive in three months, or in March.

REVERSED: *You may lavish money on domestic improvements or buy a new car, probably in March.*

[45]

♣ 2

KEY WORDS: *Avoid pooling resources.*

You may have to work twice as hard or juggle two jobs. Do not doubt your ability. Resist a temptation to solve financial problems by moving in with someone you do not love. Matters improve in February or in two months.

REVERSED: *Much to your surprise, money owed is returned to you.*

♣ **A**ce

KEY WORDS: *Extreme prosperity.*

Your professional life shines with potential. Rich acquaintances will invite you into their circles. You excel in conferences and interviews, and financial success is certain within a year. January will bring a fresh opportunity.

REVERSED: *Expect letters and papers bearing good news about exams or money.*

[46]

To find two nuts in one shell is a sign of luck in love.
Eat one while making a wish.
Give the second nut to the one you desire. It is said
to draw the person closer.

THE **HEART** SUIT

♥ **K**ing

KEY WORDS: *A passionate lover.*

Your love life is about to flourish. This Romeo
often represents the lover you are wondering
about. Genuine in his affection, he is offering love
but won't wait around forever for an answer.
Women are attracted by his charms and men enjoy
his back-slapping company.

REVERSED: *You attract a lucky love relationship, but refuse
his advances.*

♥ **Q**ueen

KEY WORDS: *A queen of romance.*

This generously loving woman is known for her
social grace. She may run charities or do voluntary
work. In marriage she is faithful, and home
and hearth are where your heart is as well. You
may introduce a new partner to your family and
friends.

REVERSED: *Someone you thought was right for you may prove
disappointing when you get to know her.*

♥ **J**ack

KEY WORD: *Cupid.*

A young man you already know, someone who is
youthful in attitude and appearance whatever his
age, is making romantic overtures. Whether you
accept his offer is your choice. Either way, romance

will radiate new light in your life, especially this summer.

REVERSED: *Whoever receives your love is lucky. Do not settle for second best.*

10

KEY WORDS: *A special new love.*

Expect a wedding invitation or news of a marriage or a birth. In ten days or ten weeks, a wonderful event will bring renewed confidence. If you have just met someone and sense love is in the air, your intuition is right.

REVERSED: *Romance could pass you by if you do not recognize an invitation.*

9

KEY WORDS: *The wish card.*

This feminine card predicts nine months of pregnancy, or the fruition of a wish, perhaps in September or on the ninth of a month. Expect a new love affair, or a passionate reunion after a period of estrangement. In delicate situations keep your wits about you and behave tactfully. Whatever you wish for, you will get.

REVERSED: *Love unbounded is dangerous and regrettable. Be cautious.*

8

KEY WORDS: *Romantic liaisons. Marriage.*

A party or a celebration yields a romantic encounter that may lead to a long-term relationship and thoughts of marriage. Family bonds are reinforced and disagreements forgiven. Expect gifts and love tokens. In August you may have a romantic holiday as a couple or with a group of friends.

REVERSED: *Love is doomed because of insurmountable obstacles.*

 7

[49]

KEY WORDS: *Contentment. Happy love.*

Your wishes for romantic love are fulfilled on the seventh of a month, in seven weeks from now, or in July. One of the most positive cards in the pack, this represents triumph over adversity and weakens the influence of any negative cards appearing on either side.

REVERSED: *A reconciliation will follow a lovers' tiff.*

6

KEY WORDS: *An amorous compromise.*

Your love life may develop slowly. A marriage proposal may be delayed. Jealousy could be an obstacle in your current relationship. During the course of events one of you will meet someone new, and you may have to choose between self-preservation and love. Six weeks or months from now, or June, will bring a change.

REVERSED: *An insincere person could present unrealistic hopes, false promises, and unreciprocated emotions.*

 5

KEY WORDS: *Loving happiness.*

You may celebrate your own happy engagement, marriage, or wedding anniversary. In spring and summer, true love will verge on perfection. There could be an inheritance of money or some other kind of support from family and friends.

REVERSED: *Someone dear to your heart will cause you grief. An estranged loved one may suddenly return.*

 4

KEY WORDS: *A strong partnership.*

Your relationship may result in the birth of two children. Two couples, or two parents and two children, will have cause to celebrate. If your relationship is experiencing a rough patch, faith and patience will see you through the next four weeks, four months, or until April, when matters improve.

REVERSED: *Unsupportive friends and family bring sudden offers of help or admiration.*

A new moon on a Saturday or

KEY WORDS: *Your wish comes true.*

You will be invited to a party where you will find romance. If you have already met someone new, a happy romance will develop. If you and your lover have parted, but you wish they would return, this card promises they will. If you are attached, your partner will continue to love you.

REVERSED: *Pleasurable flirtations and social invitations are in abundance. But someone who entices you may already be in a relationship.*

♥ 2

KEY WORDS: *A lovers' meeting.*

You may experience love at first sight and have a passionate love affair. Two hearts will beat as one, and you will be able to read your lover's mind. You can look forward to a particularly romantic evening, an intimate weekend, or a two-week holiday together.

REVERSED: *The one you love may abandon you and break your heart.*

♥ ce

KEY WORDS: *True love.*

A sparkling new life awaits you. The ace of hearts promises more to anyone in love, or in search of

Sunday is a sign of bad weather.

love, than any other card. You may decide to move in with a lover, or if you are alone, you are about to experience a powerful love. Within a month or in January, a romantic someone will send you a love letter, music, or flowers.

REVERSED: *A love affair is about to begin or grow stronger.*

[52]

THE SPADE SUIT

♠ King

KEY WORDS: *A tyrannical businessman.*

You already know, or will soon meet, an egotistical man of mature years. Ruthless in business, he inflicts misery on those who cross swords with him. He may work in the field of law. However charming, he is not to be trusted.

REVERSED: *A widower or divorcé may cross your path and cause you grief.*

♠ Queen

KEY WORDS: *An unscrupulous woman.*

A dangerous female "gold digger" could disrupt your plans. She may be widowed, divorced, or unhappily married. You need to keep safe from destructive forces, especially in October and November. And remember, "Hell hath no fury like a woman scorned."

REVERSED: *A cunning woman who creates conflicts and gossip may become a dangerous enemy.*

♠ Jack

KEY WORDS: *A well-intentioned man.*

You may be visiting a doctor, or having a meeting with your bank manager or a lawyer. You will experience relief. You may be passing exams or winning a trophy or an award. You may instead see good results after you survive a testing time.

REVERSED: *You will be faced with ordeals that you will overcome only with arduous effort.*

♠10

KEY WORD: *Disappointment.*

Failure will precede success, and right now difficulties and losses threaten. Should they materialize, single-minded determination can help you overcome all obstacles and even turn misfortune into good fortune. An argument may end your love affair or you may also suffer a short illness, but you will return to good health and spirits.

REVERSED: *Circumstances bode delays. If you are looking for employment, you will need to redouble your efforts.*

♠9

KEY WORDS: *A favorable turning point.*

Happiness, health, and peace of mind return after a trying time. A distorted part of your life is now in better perspective, thanks to a positive change you have wrought. Nine days, nine weeks, or nine months from now will bring more positive changes.

REVERSED: *Self-pity negates the inherent good that is on its way to you, perhaps in nine days or weeks. By September life will look much brighter.*

♠ 8

KEY WORDS: *Renewed hope.*

Family clashes are resolved by compromise. Romantic, business, domestic, or holiday plans may suffer hitches and delays. Friends you thought you could trust may prove unreliable or scheming. Be careful in August.

REVERSED: *You can nip a catastrophic situation in the bud. Common sense may tell you to start over.*

♠ 7

KEY WORDS: *Happiness returns.*

Luck is on your side, bringing prosperity in business and replacing conflict with love. Job prospects appear promising, though initial rewards may be small. Take solace in the positive results of your perseverance and exertion.

REVERSED: *You avoid sadness and even danger by phasing out detrimental friends and old habits.*

♠ 6

KEY WORDS: *Steady progress.*

A vast improvement, particularly in regard to your most worrying concern, is on its way. In six weeks, six months, or in June you will be viewing life differently. A critical defeat will evolve into a victory with the arrival of another opportunity.

REVERSED: *Despondency and delays before success.*

♠5

KEY WORDS: *A lovers' reunion.*

If tears have been shed over a relationship, take heart. You and your lover will be reunited. Whether to that person or another, a happy marriage awaits. Allow someone a chance to express his or her best.

REVERSED: *When your higher self governs your actions and aspirations, you are sure to attain your goal.*

♠4

KEY WORDS: *Untimely decisions.*

[56]

You have arrived at a crossroads, and have to make a choice about love or business difficulties. Romantic relationships may be emotionally fraught. Be reassured that spring will bring a new beginning, so plan your next move and look to the future.

REVERSED: *Loss of income, property, or health threatens to mar your happiness, but does not succeed.*

♠3

KEY WORD: *Heartache.*

Divorce, separation, or a broken love affair could be the result of an interfering third person or undermining situation. The loss of a friend, pet, or job may have caused upset. But brighter times return in March. You should also hear good news in three days or three weeks.

REVERSED: *Alliances are threatened, not necessarily lost.*

♠ 2

KEY WORD: *Separation.*

Plans for a change in residence, a career change, or a romantic choice may be disrupted. All three areas of your life may be affected. You may be involved in problems you did not anticipate and could lose a valuable friend. Tread carefully in February.

REVERSED: *You may discover scandal or deceit or cross swords with someone.*

♠

KEY WORDS: *Caution to avoid grief.*

Quarrels, anxiety, litigation, or bankruptcy will be the result of bad speculations or the influence of corrupt friends. However, the ace symbol on the card represents a potent, powerful new seed. A relationship may simply suffer a hitch before a flowering.

REVERSED: *Known as the death card, this augurs the final chapter of a situation, a relationship, or an investment. But remember: Every ending is a new beginning.*

[57]

THE **DIAMOND** SUIT

♦ **K**ing

KEY WORDS: *A powerful man.*

A businessman will be of practical or financial help to you, but on his terms. He encourages you to believe his help is indispensable. But beware. He may abandon you when he sees no advantage for himself. Realize you can move mountains yourself and are enjoying a winning streak.

REVERSED: *You may encounter a double-dealer in love or business.*

♦ **Q**ueen

[58]

KEY WORDS: *An approachable woman.*

You may know a flirtatious woman who entices men to fall in love with her. She will help you to solve a problem and enable you to revel in new gains and fresh hopes. You will get a chance to go somewhere you have never been before.

REVERSED: *Should there be any gossip and criticism, it will quickly fade.*

♦ **J**ack

KEY WORDS: *A man and a letter.*

You know a young man who enjoys freedom and travel. He loves you and will help your career along in numerous practical ways. A friend he introduces you to will help you to achieve your goals, but not for free.

REVERSED: *Someone you may already know wants to seduce you. But they may cause you deep unhappiness.*

♦ 10

KEY WORDS: *A journey.*

A journey, meeting, or reunion and financial luck appear likely. Someone from your past will contact you with romance in mind, but you may shun them. The tenth of a month, ten weeks from now, or October should bring renewed optimism.

REVERSED: *You may be wasting your time on undeserving people. Recognize them sooner rather than later.*

♦ 9

KEY WORDS: *Love and travel.*

You will reap a rich harvest from the seeds you have sown. Travel may lead to a new love or even greater prospects. You may move to a better job or home. An intimate friendship brightens your long-term future. In nine days, nine weeks, or in September you will begin a new phase of hard but fruitful work.

REVERSED: *You will choose how you earn a living.*

♦ 8

KEY WORDS: *Brilliant opportunities.*

Considerable profits are in store for you. They
require you to take more responsibility for your
own resources or the finances of someone close.
Good news removes doubt. Cast your net wide and
avoid putting all your eggs in one basket. You have
a holiday to look forward to in August.

REVERSED: *Someone may try to undermine your confidence.*

♦ 7

KEY WORD: *Prudence.*

Financial developments will uplift you and start you
on a new path. A contract may arrive in July, and
summer will be a happy time. Believe in yourself,
and after a while others will, too. For a time you
may have to make sacrifices for your ambitions, but
your efforts are not in vain. The next time your age
is divisible by the number seven will be the beginning of seven years' good luck.

REVERSED: *Your instincts are right.*

♦ 6

KEY WORD: *Passion.*

You may consider taking a current relationship
further, or renewing an acquaintance with someone from your past. Think twice. You will meet

charming, chatty new friends. An impending change of scenery will be either temporary or permanent. In June, you will travel to where there is water.

REVERSED: *You will make money ingeniously.*

♦5

KEY WORD: *Happiness.*

Business will be brilliant and home life will be happy. If you are unattached, a lover arrives, perhaps in five weeks' time, five months, or in May. If you are in a steady relationship, it should bring the fun and happiness you deserve. Fear of the unknown should not deter you from embracing what you want.

REVERSED: *You will be spending time with those you love.*

[61]

♦4

KEY WORD: *Compromise.*

If you are engaged in a battle of wills, you may have to strike a compromise. But have your say and do not be rendered powerless. You can and will reach the top. Good news in April will make you feel stronger. Meanwhile, you will be invited out to dinner as one of four people.

REVERSED: *You will be successful, though against all odds.*

♦

KEY WORDS: *An emotional encounter.*

If you are studying for exams, you will pass.
An influential person is singing your praises and
may persuade you to begin a new project that will
bring you a lot of respect. You will celebrate in
March as well as receive good news by telephone.

REVERSED: *Your hunches are right about distancing yourself
from unpleasant people and places.*

♦ 2

KEY WORDS: *A momentous love affair.*

Someone close will confess his or her true feelings.
You may spend a happy weekend away in February.
Pleasant company surrounds you and work brings
satisfying profits. When the daffodils are in flower,
you may hear from someone you have long
forgotten.

REVERSED: *An envious person may attempt to undermine you.*

♦ Ace

KEY WORDS: *A sparkling engagement.*

You will be laying long-term foundations, building
on them and enjoying the pleasurable way your life
develops. Your lover may pop the question. If you
are footloose, you will fall in love with someone you
will meet within a week, a month, or in January.

Alternatively, you may receive a wonderful business offer or a letter.

REVERSED: *Someone is thinking of buying you a present or asking you for a date.*

HOW TO SELECT
THE CARDS

You will need to link the individual card meanings together to get the whole picture. Consider the chosen cards separately and then as a group. If you are giving a reading to someone, shuffle the cards yourself before passing the deck to them to shuffle.

CAN I WIN
THE LOVE I DESIRE?

[64]

Shuffle the pack while thinking of the person you desire. Turn the top card faceup on the table and continue to lay the deck faceup in horizontal rows of seven cards, beginning on the left and finishing on the right. If the ace of hearts appears before the ace of spades, you will win the heart of the one you desire.

It is believed to be lucky to be born on a Sunday, to marry on a Sunday, and to begin a vacation on a Sunday.

THREE WISHES

Will my wish come true?

Concentrate on your wish as you shuffle the pack. Begin dealing the cards faceup. Bear in mind that the nine of hearts is considered the "wish card," and the ten of spades is regarded as the "disappointment card." If the nine of hearts appears before the ten of spades, your wish will be granted.

Will I get my wish?

Shuffle the pack and deal thirteen cards from anywhere in the pack. Deal them facedown on a table, then turn the cards faceup. If one or more aces appear among the cards, place the aces to one side. Shuffle the remaining cards and again deal thirteen. As before, remove any aces that appear. Repeat the process once more. If in the three deals all four aces have appeared, you will get your wish.

[65]

Will my wish be granted?

Shuffle the cards while thinking of your wish. Holding the pack facedown, remove every seventh card and place it in a separate pile. The resulting pile of seven cards will answer your question. Turn the cards faceup; if the nine of hearts (the "wish card") is among them, you will get your wish.

WILL I GET
THE MAN I WANT?

Shuffle the pack, keeping the cards facedown, while wishing for the love you desire. Randomly select thirteen cards and place them faceup in a row, beginning on the left and finishing on the right. Interpret their individual meanings, reading from left to right. ❧ Return the thirteen cards to the pack and reshuffle. Choose eleven cards and place them faceup in a row, beginning on the left and finishing on the right, as before. Then repeat the process, selecting nine cards, then seven, then five, and finally three cards. If two of these last three cards are hearts, you will win the love of the man you want.

To remove a thread of
tailor's cotton that has
attached itself to your
clothes is a warning that

WILL THAT
SPECIAL PERSON
CONTACT ME?

Shuffle the pack facedown. Ask your question as you remove seven cards from the pack. Turn them face-up. If four or more cards are red, the answer is yes. If four or more cards are black, the answer is no.

WHAT DOES
THE IMMEDIATE
FUTURE HOLD?

Shuffle the cards while holding the pack facedown. Select seven from anywhere in the pack, and lay them faceup in a row. ¶ The first card represents the present or recent past. The second card is the present or imminent future. The third card reveals even more of the future, and so on up to the seventh concluding card.

you will receive a tempting invitation or offer with strings attached.

WILL I SUCCEED
IN THIS
SITUATION?

To quickly determine the outcome of a situation or event, inquire while shuffling the pack facedown. Pick three cards, turn them faceup, and their combined meanings will give you the answer you need.

WHAT DOES
THE YEAR HOLD
IN STORE?

[68]

Shuffle the pack facedown and then select twenty-one cards. In the order in which you removed them from the pack, place the cards faceup in three rows of seven. The first card in the top row (but sometimes the second and third card too) represents current issues. The following cards and the middle row unveil the unfolding future. The last row of cards represents the more distant future.

If you drop your umbrella or walking stick, it is an omen

HORSESHOE
PAST, PRESENT, AND
FUTURE READING

From the complete deck select a card to represent the person whose fortune is being told. This is the "personal card." Choose a king or queen of hearts for a very fair man or woman. Select a king or queen of diamonds for a brown-haired man or woman. Similarly, select the king or queen of clubs if you are reading cards for a dark-haired person and the king or queen of spades for a person with black hair and dark skin. ¶ Lay the personal card faceup. Shuffle the remaining cards before passing the pack to the person who is receiving the reading. Ask that person to shuffle the pack again and then to pick thirteen cards. Beginning on the left of the personal card, place them faceup in a horseshoe shape around the personal card. The first card to appear represents the past. The following six cards represent the present. The remaining six cards disclose more distant events.

you will meet someone you know during that journey.

IS MY LOVER
FAITHFUL?

Choose a court card (i.e., a face card) to represent your lover and then return it to the deck. Shuffle the pack, then cut it into three piles. Turn the piles faceup. Fan the first pile. If the card you have chosen to represent your lover is there, read the card to the right and the card to the left of him to reveal the answer. It is likely that he is faithful if his court card is in the first fan. ❡ Look in the second and third pile if your lover is not in the first. If the court card that personifies your lover appears in the second pile, the cards are indicating that he flirts with other women. Read the two cards to the left and two cards to the right of the card that represents him. If two or more cards are red, nothing serious will develop between him and the other women. ❡ If you have to fan the third pile to find the card symbolizing your lover, he is likely to be unfaithful. To gain insight into whom he is or will be seeing, read the three cards to the left and three cards to the right of his court card.

Female cards in any row are rivals if they are next to the court card you have chosen to depict your lover.

TO CHOOSE
BETWEEN
FOUR LOVERS

Questions to ask:

Which of the four lovers will ask me out?
Which of the four lovers will be the best lover?
Which of the four lovers will make me happiest?
Which of the four lovers would be unfaithful to me?
Which of the four lovers will cause me most heartache?
Which of the four lovers loves me most?
Which of the four lovers will fulfill my wish?
Which of the four lovers is most bad-tempered?

If you are a woman asking a question, remove the four kings from the deck of cards and place them faceup in a row. Each king will personify a man of your choosing, so decide which king represents which man. If you are a man inquiring about women in his life, work with the four queens. ❧ Shuffle the remaining cards while concentrating on your chosen question. Turn the top card faceup and place it beneath the first king. You are building four columns that will run downward, so remove the second card from the shuffled deck and place it under the second king, and so on. ❧ Your question is answered as soon as you deal a card that matches the suit of the king it is underneath. After each question is answered, you may choose another question and continue dealing where you left off. ¶ When you have run out of cards, collect each of the four columns and fan them out. Compare the amount of love (hearts), money (diamonds), arguments (spades), and problems (clubs) you would have with each partner.

TO ANSWER
A QUICK QUESTION

Shuffle the pack while thinking of your question. Randomly remove one card and interpret the single card meaning for your answer.

If two people utter the same words at the same moment, the one who stops speaking first will soon receive a love letter and will marry first.

CANDLE MAGIC

A PORTENT
OF GOOD NEWS

If a candle flame emits a spark, you will receive good news coming from the same direction in which the spark flew. To determine the identity of the sender, note the wax drippings. If drips form on the right side of the candle, the sender will be male; drips on the left portend a female sender. His or her initial also may be found among the pools of wax.

SIMPLE CANDLE
DIVINATION

Light a candle with a yes-or-no question in mind. If wax drips and accumulates on the right-hand side of the candle, the answer is yes. If wax collects on the left-hand side of the candle, the answer is no.

YOU ARE
NOT ALONE

A candle that burns with a blue flame is said to indicate there is a spirit in the room.

A clump of soot on a candle wick tells that you will meet a stranger who becomes a lover.

TO DETERMINE
WHICH SUITOR
LOVES YOU MOST

A candle flame can reveal who loves you most. As you look into the candle flame, speak the name of each of your suitors. The flame will burn highest and brightest as you speak the name of the one who loves you most.

WHEN WILL
MY WISH
COME TRUE?

Light three candles, designating a time such as one month to the first candle, two months to the second candle, and three months to the third candle. The last candle to extinguish itself predicts the time when your wish will come true.

If the horns of a new moon curve slightly upward, it is a sign of imminent good weather. But if the outline

WEATHER PREDICTIONS

A candle that refuses to light is an omen of rain. Windy weather is forecast if the flame sways. A sputtering flame predicts gales and storms.

CANDLE SUPERSTITIONS

It is an omen of bad luck if a candle extinguishes itself or if a candle goes out while being carried — it forebodes an untimely ending to a situation, or a death. But if someone snuffs out a candle by accident, it is an omen that that person will soon receive a wedding invitation.

[77]

of the full moon is visible when the moon is new, it indicates rain.

Salt Superstition

If you spill salt, immediately throw a pinch of the spilled salt over your left shoulder to avoid bad luck. The salt will go into the eyes of the devil, who is said to lurk on the left-hand side of the body.

Because salt preserves food, to spill salt is an omen of a broken friendship — it foretells that the relationship will not be preserved.

To pass the salt to someone at the dining table is said to "help them to sorrow."

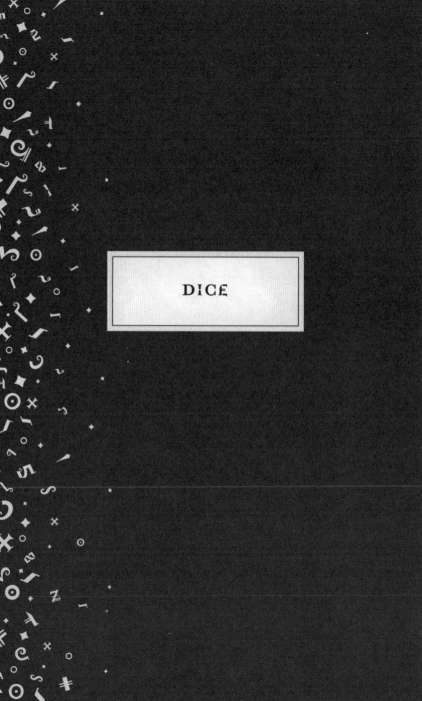

DICE

ice have been used for divination since at least 2000 B.C. The ancients divined the future by shaking and tossing two astragals, the right and left ankle bones of sheep. The name for this art of prophecy, using two dice, is astragalomancy. Using three dice for divination is called cleromancy. ❧ Tossing dice is hardly more complicated than tossing a coin for a yes-or-no answer. Fairground fortune-tellers in Victorian times used dice to forecast the future, and were known as dicers. Their practice was to throw the dice from a small wooden box held in the left hand. ❧ One or two surviving Welsh Romany Gypsies still tell fortunes with dice. They say it is lucky to blow on dice before shaking them, to blow away evil spirits. They begin by shaking the box while slowly and clearly speaking the magical words: "Ada . . . ada . . . io ada dia," as they toss dice for themselves or for a client who has thrown the dice. The phrase sounds rather like "Oh dear, oh dear, I owe, oh dear, dear." Perhaps the words have stuck to dicers who became gamblers. Whether or not you blow on the dice first and to say the words is up to you. ❧ Dicers, like many other people, know that when they ask higher forces to grant a wish verbally, it induces bestowment. But do not be fooled into thinking you will win a financial gambling bet just by uttering the dicers' potent words. ❧ Choose whether you will use two dice or three to answer a question. You might like to toss two dice before tossing three. Two dice give a prophecy; three dice not only give a prediction but also reveal character traits of the person who rolls the dice.

ASTRAGALOMANCY~ FORTUNE-TELLING WITH TWO DICE

To begin, you will need to draw a circle eleven or twelve inches in diameter on a piece of plain paper. At an outdoor party, a circle could be drawn, in chalk, on smooth pavement. ❡ To predict the answer to a question you have in mind, blow and speak the magic words "Oh dear," if you like. Then silently concentrate on your question, or ask it aloud, while shaking a pair of dice in your hand. ❡ Toss the dice into the circle. Add the number of spots facing up on both dice and refer to the table of answers. If only one die lands inside the circle, the table of answers will still apply. ❡ Here is what dice outside and inside the circle mean to the thrower. Dicers say that what is predicted will begin to come true within nine days of casting the dice.

- *One die outside the circle:* Eventually, your wishes will come true, after your own deep thoughts set wishes into motion.
- *Two dice outside the circle:* Your wish will be granted sooner than you think. Have faith. Good is on your side, bringing all you desire.

Table of Answers for a Two-dice Throw

TOTALS	ANSWERS
I	Yes.
2	No.
3	A pleasant surprise will astonish you, if you listen and behave cautiously.
4	You will be lucky when you least expect it.
5	Your wish may come true in a surprising way. Recognize and seize a golden opportunity.
6	Divine intervention will reveal the answer.
7	You will naturally win.
8	You already know the truth. To confirm your own intuition, ask for the answer to be pictured in a dream. The truth will startle you.
9	Only by a twist of fate.
10	Success is yours.
11	Stay calm and be prepared for any eventuality. Fate is on your side.
12	You will enjoy peace of mind and contentment.

CLEROMANCY~
FORTUNE-TELLING
WITH THREE DICE

Place your paper with an eleven- or twelve-inch circle on a table or flat surface. Hold three dice in your hand and concentrate on a question you would like answered. Shake the dice and toss them into the circle. ¶ If any die land outside the circle, throw them again. But on your second throw, if die again land outside the circle, dicers say you already intuitively knew the answer to your question. There is no need to throw the dice three times.

Our ancestors scratched a circle in the earth or dust on the ground to make their predictions. This may be why some say old dicers advise that dice should only be thrown when the weather is good and the prevailing atmosphere peaceful.

3	You are bold, energetic, imperturbable, and single-minded when you need to be. Qualities you possess make you very special. But sometimes you enforce your will too severely.
SINGLE WOMAN	You will have several lovers and a happy marriage after many conquests. A new lover will appear almost immediately.
SINGLE MAN	Expect to fall in love at first sight while an unexciting relationship is fading.
MARRIED	A choice still has to be made. Something or someone has to go. Two is company and three is a crowd.
4	You are a versatile, studious, and inventive achiever who looks at things logically. To those you love, you are very sensitive. But you may not enjoy as much happiness or wealth as others.
SINGLE WOMAN	You will have many frivolous love affairs, with different types of people. But your moods make some people stay away.

[85]

SINGLE MAN	While on a journey you will meet someone new who will change your life for the better.
MARRIED	You and your partner will raise a family. You should be particularly lucky in the next four months and four years. You will get a new, well-paying job.
5 [86]	You are ambitious, capable, proud, and honorable, with a strong, visionary mind. But you are your own worst enemy and can be bad-tempered.
SINGLE WOMAN	Freedom is important to you but marriage essential to your happiness. Gossip will interfere with the way you conduct your life.
SINGLE MAN	You will turn many heads and leave a trail of broken hearts. One woman you mistreat will leave you brokenhearted.
MARRIED	Quarrels and obstacles will easily evaporate.

	WHAT CASTING SAYS ABOUT YOU
6	Calm, careful, and conservative, you are a good judge of character. You love beautiful possessions but can be avaricious.
SINGLE WOMAN	You will marry into wealth but have numerous quarrels.
SINGLE MAN	After many affairs, you will eventually be lucky in love.
MARRIED	You and your partner will grow old together, lovingly.
7	Ever reliable and methodical, you will surely attain a position of responsibility at work. By being ultra-ambitious you may lose friends.
SINGLE WOMAN	You will marry a well-off man who is not always an agreeable companion. You may live to regret it and divorce.
SINGLE MAN	You will be lucky in business deals before a late marriage.
MARRIED	Potentially you are in for seven lucky months.

8		You are proud, envious, and sometimes tyrannical. You tend to live by your nerve. You can be very generous or very mean-spirited. Dicers call eight the "miser's throw." They say it's thrown by people too close to money to see much else. If a person asks if they will marry into money and eight comes up, the answer is yes.
[88]	SINGLE WOMAN	More than likely you will have only a temporary relationship with a moneyed man.
	SINGLE MAN	Driven to better yourself financially, you will be attracted to women with means.
	MARRIED	Work and ambition top your list of priorities.
9		You are strong-willed and tolerant, artistic and inspired, and tactful in word and deed. The world is your oyster.
	SINGLE WOMAN	Recurring cycles of thrift and abundance may at first delay your finding a happy relationship.

	WHAT CASTING SAYS ABOUT YOU
SINGLE MAN	It is likely that you will marry a woman above your social position. Being a wonderful lover will endear you to her.
MARRIED	Business luck and financial increases are forecast.
IO	Affectionate, witty, and determined, you also like fair play, particularly in regard to the less fortunate.
SINGLE WOMAN	It is likely that the love of your life will elude you until you have achieved a goal. You may experience solitary sorrow.
SINGLE MAN	Love comes easily to you and you will enjoy numerous trysts. One indiscreet affair could separate you from a best friend.
MARRIED	You will become well-off through work and by inheritance.

[89]

If all three dice show the same number of dots, you will shortly receive good news that will change your life for the better.

II	You are shrewd and practical and love nature. You are thoughtful and sympathetic to all living creatures.
SINGLE WOMAN	You will meet suitors with identical names, birth signs, or professions. It does not mean any of them are suitable.
SINGLE MAN	It is more than likely you will have a son before you have a daughter. A business speculation will cause you loss and legal trouble.
MARRIED	Your relationship will be mostly content and peaceful, but may lack passion if you allow it.
I2	You have a scientific mind with strong reasoning abilities. In matters of the heart you are completely sincere.
SINGLE WOMAN	You will acquire many male admirers of all ages. Some will continue to love you their entire life.
SINGLE MAN	Someone from your past will always carry a torch for you.

[90]

	WHAT CASTING SAYS ABOUT YOU
MARRIED	Neither passion nor romance will wane in your relationship.
I3	Your intellect is balanced by your innate kindliness toward others. You love order. Cheerful and honest, you are opposed to secrecy and intrigue.
SINGLE WOMAN	You will have your fair share of romance. One man you meet will enlighten you. You will recognize him because he will find you without your looking for him.
SINGLE MAN	Marriage is much closer than you imagine. You will travel shortly.
MARRIED	You will have a stroke of good luck, making your affectionate marriage more prosperous.
I4	You possess a courageous sense of purpose. No responsibility is too great for you to handle. You sometimes overestimate your powers and behave recklessly.
SINGLE WOMAN	You will receive many marriage proposals and have more good fortune than bad.

	WHAT CASTING SAYS ABOUT YOU
SINGLE MAN	You will lose nothing by waiting. You meet the one for you through an invitation.
MARRIED	Your attractive nature makes you much loved and your marriage a bed of roses.

15

You are enterprising on a large scale and have a generally optimistic outlook. Your intuitive mind is also extremely versatile. But you have a cruel streak that could land you in trouble.

SINGLE WOMAN	Even the most attractive people do not have your qualities. You are in danger of being deceived by someone you trust.
SINGLE MAN	Your generosity makes you popular. You need to exercise discretion. Someone will reveal a secret.
MARRIED	Your good humor will make the best of your life for yourself and family.

To increase your cash flow, always keep a circle of gold or green cord (to represent money) in your purse or wallet.

16	You love detail and express yourself flamboyantly. Your mind is very powerful when it is at its best. But being easily bored, you neglect putting your good qualities to use.
SINGLE WOMAN	You will receive a proposal you have long wished to hear. A welcome visitor is on his way to you.
SINGLE MAN	Your love life will be better than you ever hoped for.
MARRIED	Your marriage will be long with plenty of love and happiness.
17	You are capable of both sacrifice and forgiveness. Lovable and intelligent, you are inspired by romance. Because you are easily led, one affair may cause long-term damage.
SINGLE WOMAN	You will attain the fulfillment of your secret wish and success in your current plans.
SINGLE MAN	You will meet someone good and kind at heart but possibly difficult to live with.
MARRIED	Prosperity will knock at your door.

	WHAT CASTING SAYS ABOUT YOU
18	Your great spirituality and clarity of vision inspire you to stand by your beliefs. However, your courage will alienate you from many people.
SINGLE WOMAN	You will meet someone where you least expect.
SINGLE MAN	One lover you meet will be unlike any admirer you have known.
MARRIED	You will be entirely happy with a domestic, family-centered life and interesting work.

[94]

MARRIAGE
FOLKLORE

ENGAGEMENT RING
LUCK

+ To have a friend make a wish upon your engagement ring is lucky. But it is considered unlucky to let a friend try on your engagement ring.
+ It is also unlucky to wear an engagement ring on your ring finger before you are engaged.
+ It is luckier to have a new engagement ring than one worn by someone else.
+ A solitaire cut stone is said to indicate a solitary existence.

WEDDING BELL
OMENS

+ If three women sitting together at a dinner table possess the same initial to their Christian name, one of the three women will soon marry.
+ The first person to walk upstairs after the bride will marry next.
+ A bride who makes a wish while cutting her wedding cake will see her wish come true.
+ Placing a piece of wrapped or boxed wedding cake under your pillow is said to induce a dream of whom you will marry.

TO ENVISION
YOUR BELOVED

To see a vision of the one you are destined to marry, sit alone for one hour in a candlelit room, starting at midnight. You must have a clock or watch and a hairbrush or comb containing enough hair to remove one strand for every year that you have lived. If you are eighteen, you need eighteen strands. ❧ Remove hair strands from the brush or comb and place them in a row on a plain scarf or handkerchief that will clearly show each hair. This must be completed before one o'clock. ❧ At one o'clock, you must turn over each hair separately and say:

> *I offer my hair as sacrifice,*
> *To the one most dear in my eyes.*
> *I call on you now to come to me*
> *At this minute you I will see.*

A misty vision will appear.

A VARIATION

On October 31, light two candles on your dressing table. Stand in front of the mirror. Brush or comb your hair with one hand, eat an apple with the other. The person you are destined to marry will appear in the mirror as a vision over your shoulder. Finish the apple and snuff out the candles.

WEDDING DRESS
OMEN

Married in white you have chosen all right,
Married in green ashamed to be seen,
Married in grey you will go far away,
Married in blue you will always be true,
Married in yellow you're ashamed of your fellow,
Married in black you will wish yourself back.
Married in pink of you he'll think.

◆ It is an omen your husband will be unfaithful if you allow a friend to try on your wedding dress or outfit before you are married.

◆ You will attract wealth into your marriage by taping a coin or monetary note to the inside of your shoe so that you are standing on money when taking your vows.

◆ To marry in a church where there is an open grave is an omen of bad luck.

◆ It is considered lucky to have an even number of guests at the wedding and unlucky to have an odd number.

To see a flock of
birds in flight on your
wedding day is a sign
of fidelity and a long
and happy marriage,
blessed by heaven.

If you are a bridesmaid
more than three times,
it is an omen you will never
marry. A man who is
refused marriage
three times is said
to be a born
bachelor.

TEA LEAVES ~

TASSEOGRAPHY

Reading tea leaves or coffee grounds is extremely simple. All you need is enough imagination to see pictures in the shapes formed by clumps of tea leaves or coffee grounds. Because children are imaginative, they are especially good at it. ¶ A white cup makes tea leaves easier to see, and you must use loose leaf tea because tea bag leaves are too fine. The more exotic brands are the easiest of all to see with because the colors and dimensions of the leaves are more distinct. ¶ After pouring a cup of tea for yourself or a friend, notice if there are bubbles floating. If so, they mean kisses for you, and if they touch the rim, they augur money.

TO SEE THE FUTURE IN A TEACUP

You and your friend should drink as far down to the grounds or leaves as you can. You need to leave just enough liquid to allow the leaves or grounds to swirl around in the cup. Both of you should then turn your own cup three times, moving in a counterclockwise direction. Then carefully turn each cup upside down on its saucer to drain. Leaves or grounds left in the saucer can be read after you finish reading what's inside the teacup. ¶ Lift your cup or your friend's upright and peer into it. See what clusters of leaves or grounds have taken shape. You can move the cup around to any angle for a better look. Some leaves or grounds will appear as more than one shape, depending on how you hold the cup, so consider both symbols and their combined meaning. If you cannot see anything, try squinting. Ironically, shapes may then suddenly appear in better focus. ❦ Letters of the alphabet represent the first initial of a person's name or a place and are connected to other nearby symbols. Numbers forecast dates, days, weeks, or months of the year when events will occur. As you perceive these symbols intuitively, it is important to say aloud what comes into your mind.

Remember these tips:

+ Symbols close to the handle are events close to home.
+ Emblems facing the handle are future events.
+ Shapes facing away from the handle are past events.
+ Patterns close to the rim represent events likely to happen sooner than those at the bottom of the cup.
+ Dark leaves and grounds represent men, boys, and dark-haired people.
+ Light-colored leaves and grounds symbolize women, girls, and fair-haired people.

TEA OMENS

- It is unlucky to stir tea with anything but a spoon, and to stir someone else's tea with a spoon is said to stir trouble for them.
- If the tea you make is unexpectedly weak, it means a friendship is weakening. If it is unusually strong, a friendship is growing stronger.
- If you spill tea while making a pot, it forecasts luck for the woman of the house.
- To break a teapot is an omen of losing a loved one.
- To inadvertently place two spoons in a saucer is a sign of marriage for the person using the saucer.

Each floating leaf or ground represents a message on its way to you, from a man if they are dark colored, from a woman if light colored.

LOVE SYMBOLS

ARROW OR ARROWS: You will be smitten by love.

BED: You can look forward to a new lover or a marriage proposal, comfort and peace of mind.

BELL: Wedding bells will ring for you, a relative, or a close friend. Instead, you may be ringing in a few changes. A bell's hanging position is symbolic of heaven connecting to earth. Something important to you will receive heaven's blessing.

BOOT: Your partner changes or you change your partner.

BROOM: You will be making a clean sweep. A negative situation is being brushed aside by positive action you take.

CANDLE: Love-light. A bright new flame of passion is burning in someone's heart for you. If a relationship has recently ended, their love for you has not burned out.

CAT: Your love life will be happy. You may renew an old acquaintance.

CIRCLE: A wedding ring for you. But if you are already married, news of a wedding. A new circle of friends you meet will lead to romance.

FAN: A reference to flirtation. You should cool it. You may be involved in an embarrassing relationship and lose your good reputation.

FLOWER: A relationship will flower. A flower is symbolic of the soul and a forecast of personal happiness.

GONDOLA: You have a romantic liaison to look forward to, but you will tire of the person.

HARP: Your love life will be as sweet as heavenly music. But only after you make a change fraught with stress and tension.

HEART: You will soon fall in love. Two hearts mean you will marry. An initial, number, or symbol nearby could help develop the picture.

KNIFE: A man will visit you. But the pair of you will argue. You may sever a friendship.

NECKLACE: A necklace symbolizes bonds and ties. [107] A lover, relative, or friend may give you a necklace.

RING: You have a happy marriage to look forward to. If single, you will hear a marriage proposal.

WEALTH SYMBOLS

AIRCRAFT: An overseas business trip that brings wealth, or a vacation you can afford. If the plane is heading toward you, expect an overseas visitor.

ANT: Business success gained through your own hard work brings you in contact with like-minded people. But you will experience strong competition.

BAG: A new job that may not last long. Even if it is a brief term, the contacts you meet will bring long-term benefits.

BEE: You will be productive and as busy as a bee. You may be head-hunted. One large firm may want to keep you working for them.

BRIDGE: A bridge is symbolic of transition. It indicates that something you desire to change will change. You may be physically going over a bridge on a journey.

CAR: You will be buying a new car, or your existing car may need attention, or you will be somehow transported in luxury.

CHAIR: Your endeavors will elevate you to a more comfortable position.

GATE: Doors will very suddenly open and success beckons you.

KEY: You hold the key to someone's happiness.

LADDER: A sign that you will climb to the top in your career. The number of rungs on the ladder may indicate how many months or years it will take.

PEOPLE: Related to men, women, and children you know or have yet to meet. Interpret their actions literally. If the people are dancing, you will be going to a party. If the people appear rigid, you may hear bad news. Look for initials and numbers close by to tell you who the people are and when events will happen.

{ 108 }

A sunny January is said to predict

TORTOISE: Great financial treasures lie in store for you, but they will be slow in coming.

WHEEL: A turn of good fortune will befall you. It warns to stick to what you know and do best and to expand from there.

WINDMILL: Your hard work will soon pay off. But you may be wasting energy by looking or expending it on the wrong people in the wrong places. You need to reassess your situation.

WINDOW: Your future is looking brighter and happier. Good news on its way, or a meeting, will make you view life differently. You will also travel to mountains.

HEALTH SYMBOLS

ACORN: You have a strong constitution and will recover from any illness. You will not be ill in the future.

FROG: A sign of change from bad to good health or good to bad.

KITE: You will experience freedom and release from problems.

MOUSE: Someone who is ill will make a speedy recovery.

OAK: An oak tree or leaf is a sign that you have a strong constitution and are in good health.

frosts in March and April.

HAPPINESS SYMBOLS

ARCH: You are stepping into a brighter future but may have to battle for what you want. For some time you may have to go it alone.

BALLOON: A party balloon indicates a party invitation. A hot-air balloon reveals a special birthday present for you as well as a release from a problem or obligations.

BAT: Someone will tell you their secret. A difficult dilemma confronts you if the secret involves deceit.

BIRD: You will soon receive good news you have long wished to hear. It indicates that you will rise above your problems. The warning is not to abandon the home nest in haste.

BOOK: A bright new chapter in your life now begins if you turn over a new leaf and make some kind of positive change in your life or choice of friends.

BUTTERFLY: A butterfly is a symbol of rejuvenation. You will flirt in lighthearted company and enjoy a period of being a social butterfly.

CASTLE: Castles you have built in the air now take material form. You should expect the unexpected.

CHILD: You will have a child, or greater access to a child you may be estranged from. It is a sign of a happy future, because a child symbolizes the future and spiritual change.

[110]

CLOCK: Success. A luck opportunity arrives in regard to a project you have been planning. You will set a date for an important meeting.

CROWN: A crowning achievement will be yours. You will also gain spiritual enlightenment.

DOG: You have some faithful friends and family members. But it is also a warning to be on guard. You may also adopt a dog or look after one while its owner goes on vacation.

EAGLE: You will soar to new heights. You may become involved with an Aquarian and achieve a fresh start when the sun is in Aquarius, January 20–February 18.

ELEPHANT: An emblem of strength and wisdom, this is a reminder not to forget someone's birthday, anniversary, or special day.

[111]

FACE: You will have a face-to-face meeting with a woman (if the leaves or grounds are light colored) or with a man (if they are dark). Lots of faces indicate social meetings or work conferences.

FISH: Symbolic of a wealth of friends and power, this indicates news from a distance or even overseas.

FLAG: A flag means victory; you will assert and establish yourself.

HORSE: You will travel speedily to somewhere new.

HORSESHOE: You will be lucky.

HOUSE: Good news will land in your mailbox. A welcome visitor will call. You will move to a new home, if that is your plan, or you may work on home improvements.

JESTER: You will be invited to a celebratory event, possibly when the sun is in Gemini, May 21–June 21. A Gemini-born person might be the one to invite you. You may have to sacrifice one thing for the sake of something else.

LEAVES: You will be successful and happy—the more leaves, the better.

LETTER: You will sign important documents. An initial nearby may indicate the sender.

MAN: You will meet a man in five days, five weeks, or five months from now. When the sun is in Taurus, April 20–May 20, a lucky change will occur. A man whose birth sign is Taurus could alter your lifestyle.

MOON: A sign that you are clairvoyant. If the moon is new (with its curve to the right and pointed ends to the left), a new opportunity will arrive for you when the next new moon appears in the sky. If the moon is old (with the curve to the left and pointed ends to the right), a situation or person will depart from your life when the next old moon appears in the sky. As an emblem, it warns to be especially careful not to make mistakes when the moon in the sky resembles the moon in your cup.

PARCEL: Expect a gift. An initial close by may reveal from whom.

SCALES: You will be victorious, particularly where legal matters are concerned, if the scales are balanced. If the left-hand side is up, you will first experience frustration. If you are trying to lose weight, the scales are a sign of your success.

SCISSORS: You will probably be drawn into a quarrel or may see others split up or move away.

SHIP: Your ship is coming in. You will travel abroad. But if the vessel looks shipwrecked, you are in for a stormy time and your life may suffer a bit of a battering.

SHOVEL: You will be preparing the groundwork for something big, which requires your physical exertion.

[113]

SPOON: You will be tasting the sweet life and will also receive a christening invitation.

SUN: Cheerful news will fill your heart with sun-shine and warm your life. You will also be taking a sunshine holiday.

WOMAN: A woman alone signifies that you will meet a woman of importance to you and through her, new friends. A group of women signifies scandal or deceit among women you trust.

TO DOWSE
A YES-OR-NO
ANSWER

This ritual can give you a yes-or-no answer about something you have seen in the cup when reading the leaves or grounds. Use the cup you have drunk from, or else use an empty cup or drinking glass. ¶ Inside the rim, suspend a plain ring by a length of cotton or fine thread held between your thumb and your index finger. Ask your question. The ring will swing and tap the inside of the rim once for yes and twice for no.

[114]

If a moth encircles you
or a light at night, it is
a sign a letter or parcel is
on its way to you.

BAY LEAF MAGIC

WILL I BE
VICTORIOUS?

A bay leaf can help you predict which person in a group will be successful in a certain endeavor. ¶ Take as many bay leaves as there are people present. Using a pen or pencil, mark the back of one leaf with a cross. Place the bay leaves in a dish. Ask a simple question such as: "Who among us will next win some cash?" All participants should then close their eyes, and in turn select a leaf from the dish. The person who picks the leaf marked with a cross is the one.

BAY LEAF
DIVINATION

To receive an answer to a yes-or-no question, ask your question aloud while holding a bay leaf to a candle flame. If the leaf crackles while burning, the answer is yes. If the leaf bubbles or makes a squeaking noise, the answer is no.

Ruled by the sun
and sacred to Apollo,
bay symbolizes victory.

TO DIVINE
YOUR LOVER'S
FAITHFULNESS

With a pin, scratch your lover's initials or name on a fresh bay leaf. If the letters remain green throughout one day, it is unlikely the person in question is faithful. If within a day the initials or name turn brown, your sweetheart is true. If the initials or name are more clearly marked than when you wrote them, it is an omen that you will marry each other.

WHICH OF MY
WISHES WILL COME
TRUE FIRST?

Pick three bay leaves to symbolize three wishes. With your wishes in mind, place the bay leaves on a table, and place a candle in a holder upon each leaf. Speak one wish aloud as you light each candle. The first candle to burn out indicates which of your three wishes will be the first to come true.

TO DREAM OF
THE ONE
YOU LOVE

Take five fresh bay leaves and five safety pins. Pin one
bay leaf to the center of your pillow and the remaining four bay leaves to each corner. Turn the pillow
over so the bay leaves are underneath. During the
night you will dream of your future lover.

[119]

Should you unintentionally
say something that rhymes,
        it is a sign you will soon
hear extraordinary news
    that affects you personally.

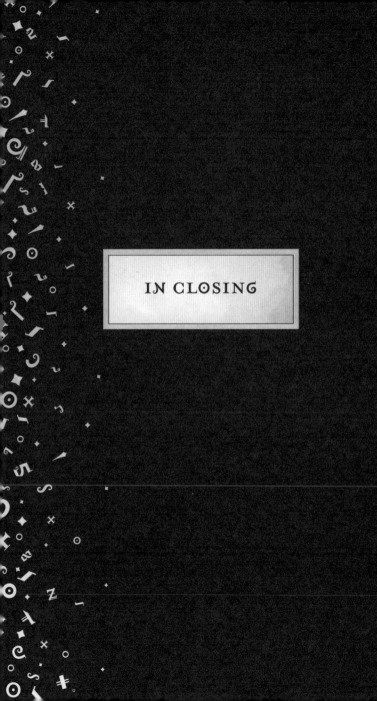

IN CLOSING

FOR A WISH
TO COME TRUE

When you see
a shooting star,
make a wish before
the star fades.
It will come true.

You should
also make a wish when
you see a rainbow.
But remember:
Never tell
your wish.

And so from reading a crystal ball to playing cards and dice, to reading tea leaves and coffee grounds, we can see omens in everyday life. ❡ Beautiful and wonderful things do happen, we attract them to us by living in the hope and expectation of them. May all the good you predict for yourself and others come true. And may all that you wish for come true, too.

[123]

FIRST EDITION

Book design by Julia Sedykh Design

Library of Congress Cataloging-in-Publication Data
Kemp, Gillian
The fortune-telling book : reading crystal balls,
tea leaves, playing cards, and everyday omens of love
and luck / by Gillian Kemp. — 1st ed.
p. cm.
ISBN 0-316-48835-6
1. Fortune-telling. I. Title

BF1861 .K46 2000
133.3—dc21   00-035662

Q-TN

10 9 8 7 6 5 4 3 2

Printed in the United States of America

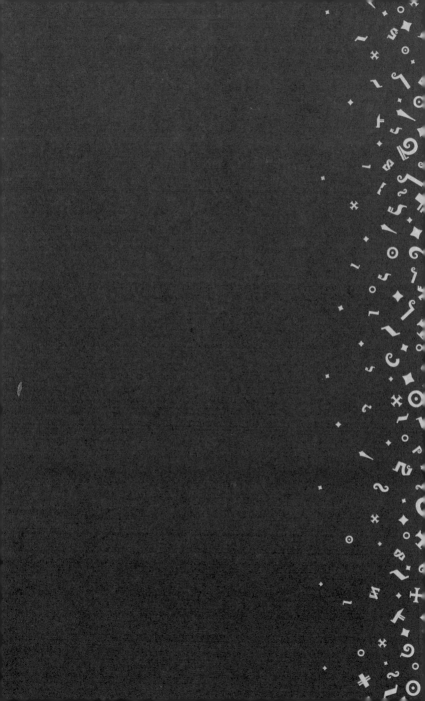